NATURE IS FUN!
ALL ABOUT NATURE FOR KIDS
THE FOUR ELEMENTS

BABY PROFESSOR

EDUCATION KIDS

Speedy Publishing LLC
40 E. Main St. #1156
Newark, DE 19711
www.speedypublishing.com

NATURE

Nature is
everything
that people
did not make.
A physical
world that has
everything
in it.

It includes us, plants, animals, mountains, oceans and stars. It lives between us or as a part of the human activities .

The ancient
Greeks
believed that
there were
four elements.
And that
Everything
was made
up of earth,
water, air,
and fire.

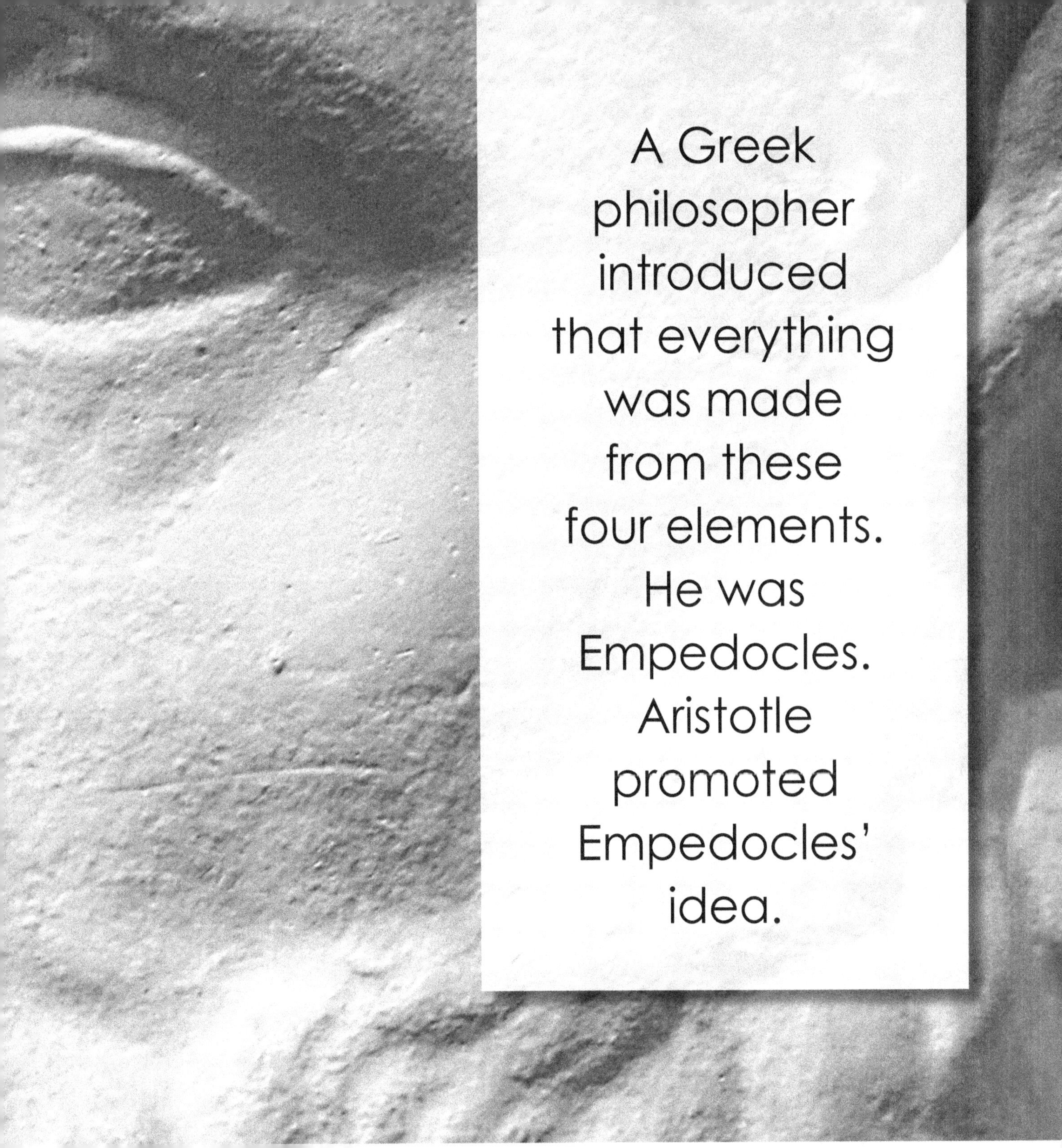

A Greek
philosopher
introduced
that everything
was made
from these
four elements.
He was
Empedocles.
Aristotle
promoted
Empedocles'
idea.

The four
elements
supports the
four states
of matter
in modern
science. Solid
is to earth,
liquid is to
water, gas
to air and
plasma for fire.

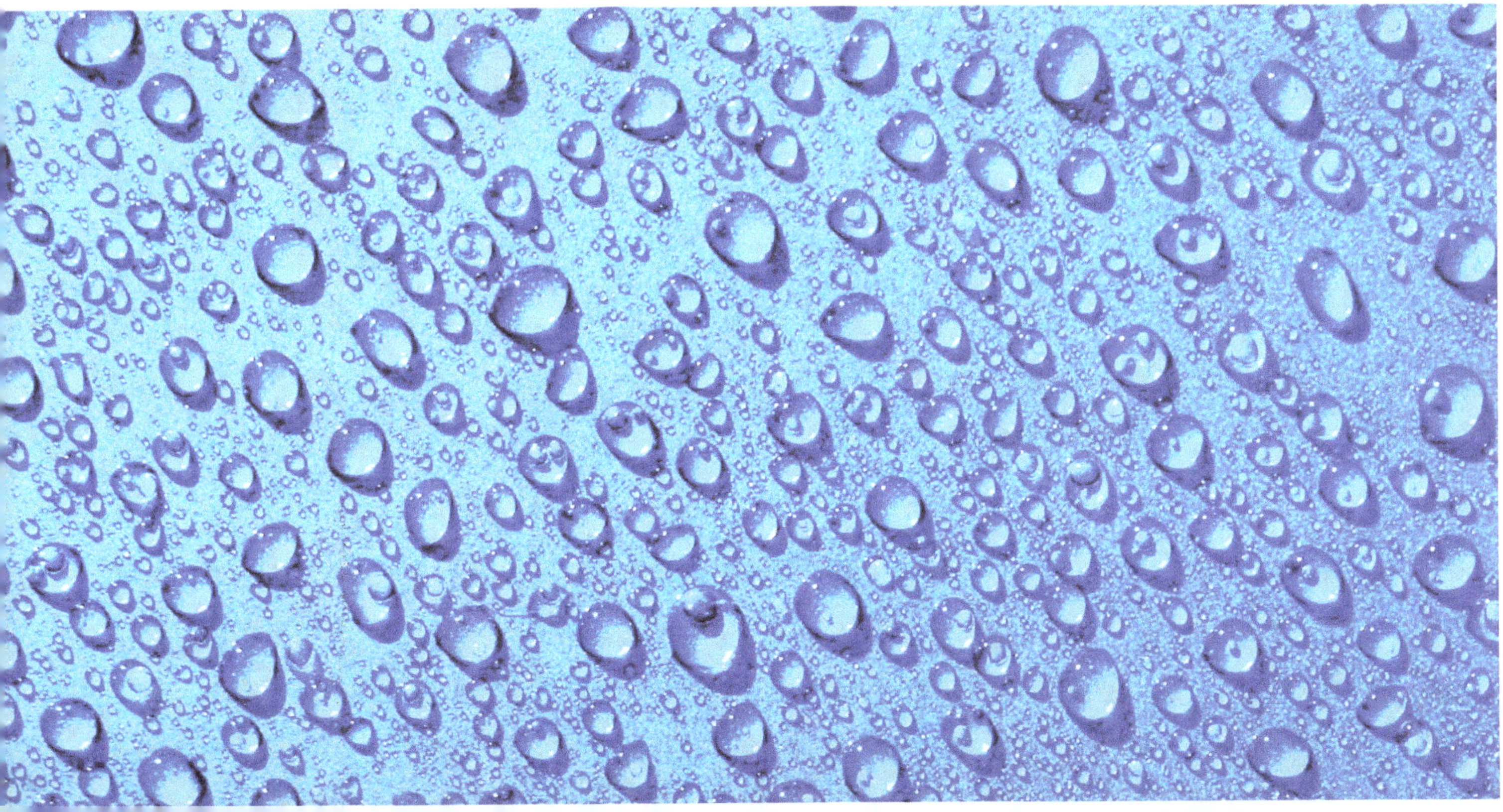

It was also
thought
the the four
elements
are placed
naturally. And
when mixed
or combined,
they can
appear in to
Something new.

The classical
elements of
science are
earth, water,
air and fire.
They are old
beliefs but
we can still
experience
them today.

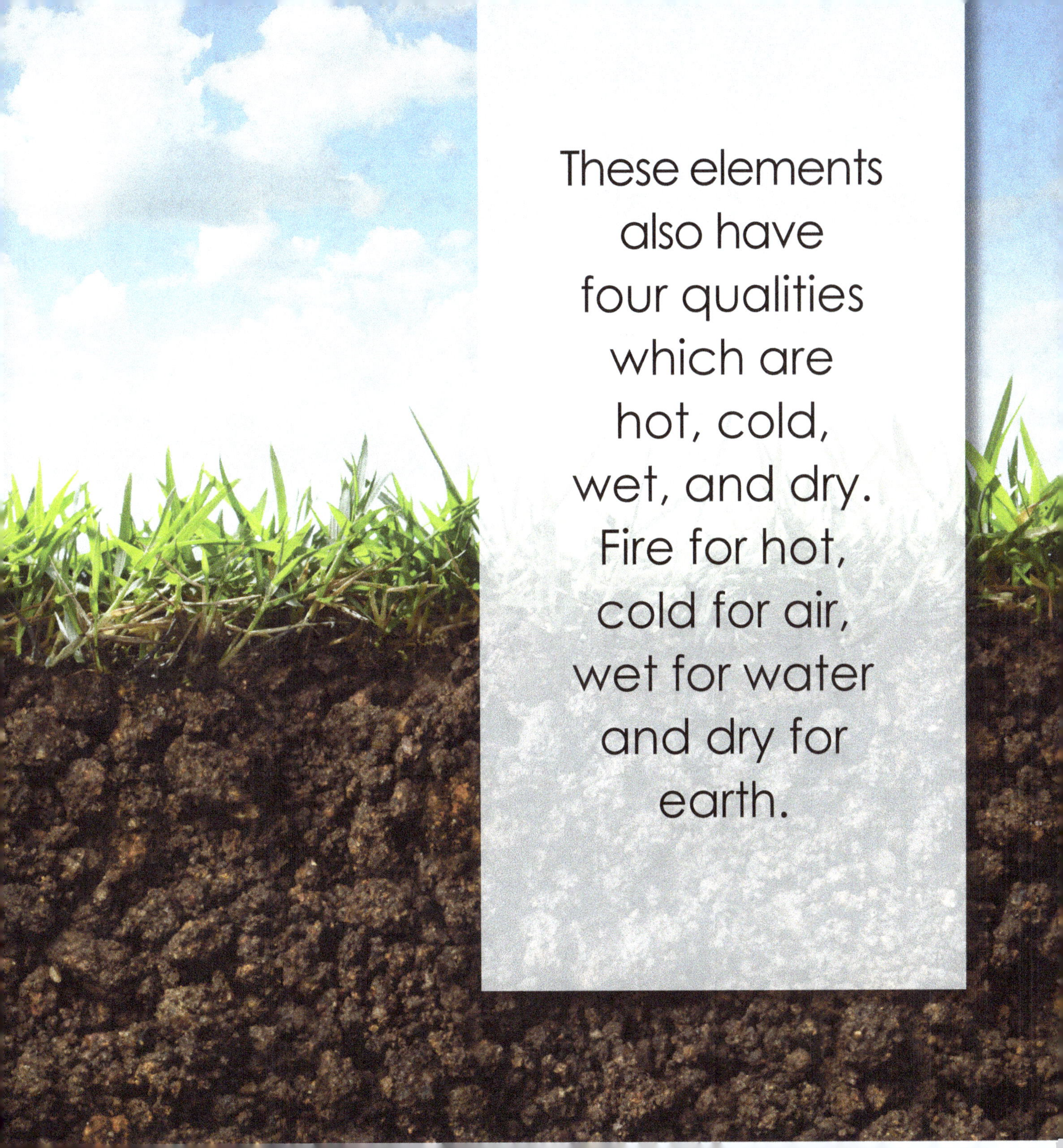

These elements
also have
four qualities
which are
hot, cold,
wet, and dry.
Fire for hot,
cold for air,
wet for water
and dry for
earth.

We think of
Earth as solid
and dirt. But
the Earth is
made up of
several layers.
It has different
kinds of rocks
and minerals.

Earth gives soil to grow plants and support life. Earth is commonly related with the colors brown and green.

Many rocks
contain
calcium,
and oxygen
Some have
aluminum
too. The
Earth's crust
contains iron.

Rocks and stones are natures living solids made up of minerals. Metamorphic rocks like marble, are created by extreme pressure and heat.

The colors blue, white, yellow or gray are associated with Air. Air is invisible and often considered as a pure element. Air is life.

Without air
we can't live.
We breathe
oxygen
and release
carbon
dioxide for
plants to use.
Plants create
oxygen and
the cycle
goes around.

Air is all
around us
and is made
up of different
gases. These
are nitrogen
and oxygen.
These gases
are just right
for life on
Earth.

There is also
air that is bad
for us and our
planet. The
polluted air. It is
contaminated
by harmful
matters.

Polluted air
can cause
health
problems.
It can
damage the
environment.
Our homes,
trees and
lakes won't
be safe.

Water as we
all know is
blue in color.
It has qualities
of wetness
and coldness
in ancient
Greek times.

Water is
recognized as
the universal
solvent
because it
can dissolve
many things.
Water is
considered to
be the most
important
substance on
our planet.

There are different states of water. Water can turn solid in the form of ice. Water turns to gas, or vapor, when it is heated.

Water is vital to the human body. The ocean, rivers, animals and plants needs it too. All living things need water to survive.

About 75% of the Earth is covered with water. Most of the water is in the oceans. Did you know that a person can live for around a month without food, but not without water.

The element
of fire creates
light and
heat. Fire is
related to the
colors red or
orange. And
its qualities
were both
heat and
dryness.

Heat, fuel and oxygen are the necessary elements to start a fire. Heat is also needed to maintain or spread fire.

Fuel is
characterized
by any kind
of material
that can be
flammable.
Oxygen
supports the
chemical
process for
fire called
combustion.

Fire is very dangerous, especially to kids. It is very important to get help from grownups when using fire.

Did you know that forest fires are very dangerous for humans and animals? Forest fires are uncontrolled and difficult to stop. It can damage the environment.

Humans also use fire for light, heat, cooking and more. Scientists think that humans began using fire to cook food in a regulated way around 1 million years ago.

These
elements
represent
energy and
symbolize
distint
personalities
of human life.